Love? Lust? Lunacy?

In a Lunch Box

Richard B. Logan

AuthorHouse™
1663 Liberty Drive
Bloomington, IN 47403
www.authorhouse.com
Phone: 1-800-839-8640

Published by AuthorHouse 8/31/2012

ISBN: 978-1-4772-5719-7 (sc)

Library of Congress Control Number: 2012912792

This book is printed on acid-free paper.

Dedication

To Jann:

My Muse:

Without you the words would never have been felt.

To Jan:

My Friend:

Without you the words would not be read.

To Lee and Kelly Barrows:

Thank you for your patience, talents, opinions, and O.C.D.

Without you the words could not be read.

To Elizabeth (Mom):

Without you I simply would not be.

Info Notes

References to Andrew, Waifs, BJ and the "boys" are Jann's adopted son, his friends, BlackJack her panther-like watchcat and a grouping of any of them.

No Time!
You're Here -
You're Ready To Go.
You're Lovely -
You're Wanted -
You're Loved -

Yours.

♡ ♡ ♡
♡ Richard
♡ ✗ ♡
✗ ✗

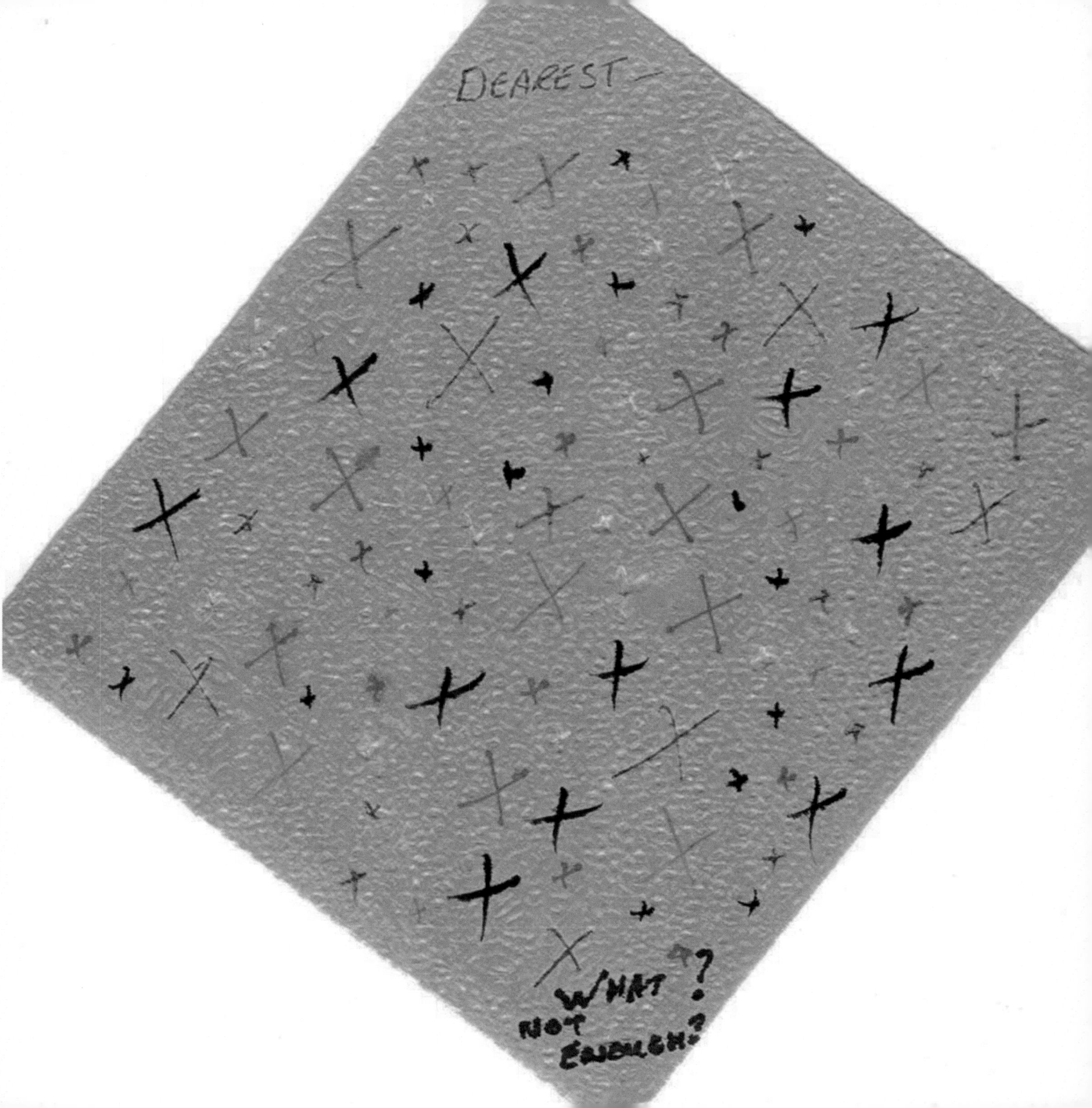
DEAREST –
WHAT?
NOT ENOUGH?

Hello, Love

Another weekend
has just flashed on by.
We got some things accomplished
I think, with a sigh —
Your presents are done — and decorations
are done —
Our Pre-Christmas week will
be nothing but fun —
Even on this positive note —
You should know there's
something I've missed —
It's that wonderful feeling
I get when I know
I've been kissed —
By You —
afg

Darling,
Jann.

Waking was
Wonderful - thank You
It only gets better -
I got to watch your face -
no lines - no worries smooth -
ageless - beautiful - a pleasure -
a boost to my pride - a melting of
my heart - a feast for my eyes -
Hope your day puts a smile on your
face - looking forward to seeing
you this evening - studying
together and cuddling
to sleep -
I love
you
x R x
R

My Darling,
Jawn,

With the end of
the month rushing
towards us, all I can think
of is having enough time
to snuggle to our hearts and
body's content - if we did nothing
at all after you retired, but snuggle, I would
be in Heaven - To get to do all we plan
and snuggle - well - the best of every
world -

May your day smile -
as mine does when I think
of you -
All my love -

Richard
♂&♀

My DARLING,

Seems like eons
since I wrote to you —
There are a lot of new
memories —
Thank you for the beach, and the
sun and no clothes in the wind and
your body and the bonfire and the stars
and the sights along the way and your body
and the beautiful Christmas House and the
home smells and your body and your
snuggles, snores, and softness of your sk
and your smiles and your 2 - step
and your cuddles on the
couch and our love —

Kiss me — Just as
soon as you
can —
♡ Always ♡
x
♡ Richard
xx

Jann, My Love,

I missing you—

Just to sit and giggle or cuddle while watching a movie — I guess I feel it more on Fridays as the week has shot by and we can still think of too much to do— or could it just be that little sadness at having to say goodbye all over again— you'd think I'd get used it _____ NEVER!

I'm Loving you more and
x more—
♡ Richard x
v

DEAR HEART,

I WATCHED YOU SLEEP FOR A LONG TIME, LAST NIGHT -

YOU ARE TRULY BEAUTIFUL - LONG, GOLDEN, WONDERFUL CURVES, NOT A LINE ON YOUR FACE - REMARKABLE! I AM A VERY LUCKY MAN - AND YOU ARE MOST PLEASING TO THE EYE - I LOVE LOOKING AT YOU - I LOVE BEING WITH YOU - I LOVE YOU

x ♡ x
♡ RICHARD
x x

Hello Darling—

I've got to say—

Sleeping wrapped around
you, in you, and next to
you only gets better and
better and harder and harder
to pull away in the mornings.
I'm sorry I was late getting up—you just
feel so good—early tonight—please!

Hoping for a flying day—

Loving you

Richard
xx

Pixie Face,
Nymphette Body
Elven Eyes
Sylphe Psyche -
The stuff Ancient
Legends Are made of -
From the days when Ageless
Forests covered the Earth - when
Every glade was a sanctuary and every
Stream spoke as it passed by -
The memories and images you
invoke are an ever surprising
source of wonder -
The Imagination of my Heart
soars on wings of Age old
Remembrances - all from
loving and being loved
By. you -
- Always
♡ Yours ♡
Kehhned
x x

Good Day
To You, M'Lady.

Another week has
come and gone —
And as with all the rest
we've had, this one too, was
a lot of fun —
Giggling in the kitchen - sharing
our meals - studying to gether -
Pleased with our christmas deals -
I know I've said before - And I will,
Again and again - Thank you —
Without our love my
existence could never
be the same —
I love
x x you — x

SNUGGLE-BUNNY

IF IT IS AT ALL
POSSIBLE FOR YOU TO FEEL
BETTER & BETTER WITH EVERY
SNUGGLE, EVERY MORNING - YOU DO IT.
IF IT'S NOT POSSIBLE, THEN YOU
ARE ACCOMPLISHING THE IMPOSSIBLE RIGHT
HERE, IN OUR OWN LITTLE PATCH OF TEXAS.
I WILL BE COUNTING MY YEARS WITH YOU IN
TERMS OF HOW MANY TIMES I WAKE AND
SEE YOUR FACE AND FEEL YOUR BODY—
FOR ME ITS THE BEGINNING OF EACH
POSSIBILITY FILLED DAY AND I
LOOK FORWARD TO IT—

FOREVER, SNUGGLING

LOVING ALWAYS
♡
RICHARD
? x x

Dearest of all -
my day smiles
waking to your face.
my heart beats that
much stronger with the
thought that you have
been lying naked next -to me
all night - my first instinct is to
always touch you. Just to
be sure all is real.
I can imagine being other places
doing other things - living another
life. But there's always this
bloody great blank spot.
and I don't want to
live with that -
I'm glad you
are here.
x L x

My Princess,

Holding you as I
sleep makes such a
difference - I sleep better,
I dream better, I'm at home
with you - I need to be wrapped around
you for my continued well-being - I
need the closeness and scent of you
in my every sleeping breath -
'strangely enough - you don't
snore as much when we're
holding each other -'

Looking
Forward
To tonight -
I Love
x You
x R x

My Love,

From the
rising of the
sun accompanied by
the singing of birds
to the appearance of the
moon and stars with all their
descriptive words—

From mountain passes, river valleys
and endless grass plains glistening

with dew—

There is nothing more, beautiful

satisfying or natural

than being in love

with and living

my life

with you—

R

Princess,

You are warmer and closer than ever - you live in my heart - inhabit my soul and are a permanent resident in my mind. I could no more not live with you than breath - I do feel we are meant for us and each other - being next to you is as natural as life. Living with you as normal as sunrise. And loving you as wonderful as coffee and cuddles in bed on a rainy, non-work day. As ever.

♡ Yours ♡

xP.

Cheek to Cheek
Nose to Nose.
Breath to Breath
Heart to Heart
Soul to Soul _____

That's our sleep dance and
You are the best partner I've
ever shared the rythms of the
night with -
Our bodies find their own steps
and fit perfectly - cat or no cat -
You will always be right for
my body - my sleep - my dreams -

Your Love -

Richard x

♥ zzzzz
x

My Love

Closer and closer,
Minute by minute,
Hour by hour,
Day by Day — all leading
To our Liberation and
PLAYTIME !!! You've worked
Really hard and can be proud - we
can be proud. I am proud of you.
We've done a lot. But its just
Confirmation that, together,
there isn't much we can't
Accomplish together. Soon.

Sweetheart, the light
is in sight - the Tunnel
has an end - and we
have another
Beginning -
Yours &
x R x

My Love,

Again, that time has come all too soon - missing you, as always. The day will be too long, not seeing you or touching you, at will, will be frustrating, fantasizing will, again, become a resource and picturing you at work will be my recourse - dreaming of you home soon - loving you as always -

Yours
x ♡ x
Richard
♥ ♥ ·

Princess,

Thank you.

For taking such good care of me - It's taking some getting used to and, I'm sure, a little like pulling teeth for you, but, after I've been hog-tied and slapped down I alway end up feeling better, healthier, and a little subdued.

I trust placing my heart and body in your care like I've never trusted before and it feels right. You feel right, we feel RIGHT —

Yours only
for Always —
♡ ♡
Richard
x x

My Love,
My HEART,
My DARLING,
My FRIEND,
My PARTNER,
My MOST WANTED,
My SHARED SOUL, My COMPANION,
My PLAYMATE, My HERO, My TEACHER
— My LOVER —

I miss your BODY AND ALL IT DOES
To MINE — SOON.?

Yours
Only

Richard
x
x

My Darling,

So Much
So Soon
So Little Time -
So What?

We Are Together - We
Will Be Together - We Can Do
All We Set Out To Do -
I Would Set Out On This Part Of
My Life With No One But You -
Without Fear - Without
Doubt - Without Regret -

With Love -
Always -

Richard
♡ xxx

Hello Princess —

A DAY TO SNUGGLE,
AND WRAP EACH OTHER
IN OUR BODIES —

I WAS THIS .. CLOSE TO DRIFTING
BACK TO DREAMLAND, WITH MY
NOSE NESTLED IN YOUR NECK AND
MY LEG DRAPED OVER YOUR THIGH —

WHAT A PERFECT FIT YOU ARE —
I'll BE KIND OF DREAMY TODAY —
I USUALLY AM WHEN FEELING LIKE
THIS — I'll BE KEENLY AWARE OF
YOUR ABSENCE AND I'll MISS YOU —

THINKING
DREAMING
WANTING
❤ OF YOU —
LOVINGLY —

√R×

My Heart,
I could caress
your face and body
with my eyes for the
rest of my life—you
are sleek, golden, smooth
and curvy in all the right
places—

You carry yourself with bearing
any self-respecting princess, with
class, would. I am proud and
honored to love you—to be
loved by you—to live
my life with you—

—ALWAYS—

RICHARD xx
♡ ♡
♡

My Love,

Another day
Living with you has
Turned into another
Night by your side has
Turned into another
Morning not wanting to leave
And softness of your body has turned
Into have a wonderful morning
The warmth has turned
Iii miss you, I'm thinking of you
And I'm looking forward to your
Face this evening —

Loving you —
x Marie —
♡

Richard ♡
♡ x ♡

My Love.

The closer we
get to leaving. The
more I want to be alone
with you —
I think I need to just
have you to myself for a little
while — I miss being lost in you —
I always seem to know where I am
when that happens —
Another wonderful contradiction
of loving you —
see you this evening,
lover.

Yours &
Richard
x x

My HEART,

My SOUL,

My LOVE,

THANK You FOR YOUR CARING

THANK You FOR YOUR FEELING OF 'US'

My BODY WANTS MORE - My HEART FEELS

MORE - I AM MORE - OF You - FOR You -
BECAUSE OF YOU -

I LOVE You - DON'T EVER LET ME

FORGET IT AND I WILL ALWAYS

REMIND You -

ALWAYS -

RICHARD x x

My Love

This was one
of those supersonic
weekends - Saturday
seems like years ago and
Sunday was a blink of an eye -
its getting really strange - at least
this week will be shorter -
working wise - and we can get
away. It doesn't seem like we've
spoken much lately - is that another
Einstienian effect? or am I
just being extra-sensitive?
Musings for a
Monday -
Home soon
my darling
x R x

My HEART
My LOVE -
My FRIEND -
Thank You FOR YOUR
COMPANY THIS WEEKEND -
I ENJOYED YOU - WONDERFULLY.
I SEEM TO BE REALLY LOOKING
FORWARD TO THEM, NOW, MORE THAN
EVER - OR IS IT YOU I LOOK FORWARD TO ?
EITHER WAY - AS LONG AS WE'RE
TOGETHER I'm HAPPY -
I JUST KISSED YOU -
I WANT MORE - !
& MORE - -
LOVE AS
♡ EVER -
x♡ R ♡x♡

M'LADY.
DARLING —
DOLLFACE —
SWEET THING
SWEETCHEEKS
SNUGGLE BUNNY
CUDDLE BUNNY
MY LOVE
MY HEART
BEAUTY
SWEETHEART.

THE LIST OF NAMES JUST KEEPS ON GROWING.
ALL YOU. ALL CHARACTERIZING A WAY
I FEEL ABOUT YOU. ALL FROM THAT
PLACE THAT GROWS EVERYTIME
I LOOK AT YOU —
I GUESS THAT MAKES YOU
EITHER FERTILIZER
OR THE SUN?
LOVINGLY —
SK

My DARLING -

IT IS NOT ENOUGH
TO JUST WISH YOU A
WONDERFUL DAY - I MUST
WRITE IT -
IT'S NOT ENOUGH TO THANK YOU
FOR ALL YOU ARE AND DO TO ME -
I MUST REPEAT IT OVER AND OVER.
IT'S NOT ENOUGH TO LIVE UNDER THE
SAME ROOF - I WANT IT TO BE OUR
HOME - IT'S NOT ENOUGH TO
TELL YOU I LOVE YOU -
I WANT TO SHOUT IT -
ALWAYS WILL
NEVER BE
ENOUGH -
" R "

PRINCESS TO
my HEART –

YOU ARE ALL I COULD
EVER WANT – AND MORE THAN
I WOULD EVER NEED

AFTER EACH NIGHT IN YOUR ARMS – MY HEART
AND SOUL FEEL SET FREE –

I LOVE YOU JANN – MORE THAN I
COULD EVER SAY –

YOU FILL MY LIFE WITH BEAUTY
EVERY LOVING DAY –

THANK YOU –

YOURS, MINE,
& OURS ♡
x
R

My love,

Another wonderful waking time with you -
Marking milestones with you in terms of opening my eyes in the morning and feeling your arms around me or seeing your face has become an everyday anticipated pleasure - I'm thankful - everyday - and glad it's you -

I'm feeling quite tender this morning and would love to cuddle - so that will be the basis of todays dreamy thoughts of you - until tonight, sweetheart -

Great day -
Loving you -
Richard
X ♥ X

My Sadie Hawkins

Some might believe
it's your clear blue eyes
and open smile -
Others, the softness of your skin
and the beauty in your face -
Some would say it's your sense of right
coupled with your classy style
and others still, your love for all and your
respect for everyones' personal space.
For me its all of the above and so
very much more.
Even after I add to that - your
intelligent wit and winning charms
my wish for Sadie Hawkins day
knowing what's in store -
is a lifetime of
leap years
waking in
your ♥
arms ♥
♥ R ♥

My HEART,

ANOTHER MORNING.
DRAGGED KICKING + SCREAMING
FROM YOUR ARMS —
LEFT TO CARRY-ON — PERSEVERE
AND GENERALLY MAKE IT THROUGH
ANOTHER DAY. UNTIL YOUR FACE
BRIGHTENS THE HOUSE AGAIN —
IS IT ALREADY DOES MY HEART —

HOPE THE DAY FLIES FOR YOU —

I'll MISS YOU —

I LOVE YOU —

I'M YOURS —

RICHARD

DEAREST,
HEART —

To WAKE WITH you —
  IS THE BEGINNING of
          LIFE —
To WORK WITH you —
  IS THE WANT IN LIFE
To PLAY WITH you — IS MY JOY IN
                    LIFE —
To LIVE WITH you — IS AS NATURAL
                    AS LIFE —
To TOUCH you — IS MY NEED IN LIFE —
To LOOK AT you IS A REWARD OF LIFE

      To LOVE you IS LIFE —

          ALWAYS —

          RICHARD
            xx

My Love,

This is it!

Final Day!

You have done it!

I'm very proud of you.

You've done a great job.

And no matter what 'Little Napoleon'

has to say you will always be

my 'Honor Graduate' —

Our first completed Concrete Step

Towards our future —

Accolades all around

Looking forward to

our celebratory

weekend —

& As ever —

~ R ~

My Love,

I'M GLAD THIS
WEEK IS SHORT.
I'VE GOTTEN USED TO
BEING AROUND YOU AND
HEADING BACK TO WORK IS A
BIT LONELY ALL OVER AGAIN.
I KNOW THE EXAM AND GALAPAGOS
WILL BE JUST AROUND THE CORNER
AND THAT WE HAVE WORK TO DO.
I'M HAPPY THAT YOU ARE THE ONE I GET TO
DO IT WITH. TODAY WON'T BE
SO BAD WITH YOU BEING ABLE
TO COME HOME AND
TOMORROW IS ONLY
1 DAY. YOU ARE
WANTED &
LOVED
x R x

To My -

HEART OF HEARTS.

SHARED SOUL & FRIEND.

THANK YOU EVER SO MUCH

FOR THIS MOST EXCELLENT

WEEKEND —

THANK YOU FOR THE LOVE, THE LAUGHTER

YOUR BODY AND ALL ITS' WONDER -

ALL IN ALL - A HALLOWEEN THAT WAS

TRULY A TREAT -

ALTHOUGH, OUR LACK OF GHOULISH

VISITORS LEAVES US WITH LOTS

OF SWEET THINGS TO EAT —

BON APPETITE —

LOVING
YOU

x
x Richard x
x

My Love,

All I have

This morning is —

Thank You —

Thank you for a wonderful weekend — I'm proud to step out with you — whether it's a funky band in a bar or chamber music at the university — you grace everything, including my heart. with your presence.

Loving you more and more. always and all ways.

— until tonight —

♡ ✗ ♡

✗ Richard ✗

♡ ✗

My DARLING -

KNOW THERE IS
NO-ONE I WOULD
RATHER SPENT TIME
WITH - HOLD - KISS - SLEEP
WITH OR LOVE THAN YOU
KNOW THERE IS NO-ONE TO
HOLD - HAVE - AND CHERISH MY HEART
AS YOU DO - KNOW THERE IS NO-ONE
I TRUST AND RESPECT AS I DO YOU
KNOW ALL THIS AS I DO -
YOU ARE FOR MY LIFE
I AM FOR OURS -
MY HEART
IS FOR YOU -
RICHARD
x

My DARLING, Sann,

HERE'S TO YOU, -
HERE'S TO ME -
HERE'S TO US -
WITH APPRECIATION
WITH GRATITUDE
WITH RESPECT
WITH LOVE
WITH LUST
WITH ALL MY HEART, BODY AND SOUL
YOU ARE WANTED
YOU ARE CHERISHED
YOU ARE ADORED
YOU ARE MY
BEAUTY/ -
ALWAYS
8 R x x

Dearest Jann,

You are right,
I don't have to
write a note everyday.
I don't have to kiss your
face every morning. I don't
have to make sure you have
a lunch. I don't have to be
your friend. I don't have to relieve
you of your household chores.
I don't have to be here. I don't
have to spend my life with
you. I don't have to care
about you. I don't
have to love
you —
I want to.!!
♡ J ♡

DARLING,
DAWN,

WORDS TO EXPRESS
THE PLEASURE OF
SPENDING TIME WITH YOU,
UNINTERUPTED, WILL ALWAYS
BE INADEQUATE, EINSTEINIAN,
IS ONE - THE LAST 5 DAYS HAVE
FLOWN - SATURDAY NIGHT STRETCHED
A BIT, BUT MONDAY AND TUESDAY
CAUGHT IT UP AND ZOOMED BY-
I LOVE THE TIME WITH YOU - I
ALWAYS WILL - I LOVE YOU - FOR
EVEN LONGER - I LOVE YOU -
UNTIL THERE IS NO
TIME -
RICHARD

Darling,
Jawn,

In my HEART
of my SOUL
In my DREAMS
of BEING WHOLE

In my EYES
Your BEAUTY SHINES

In my MIND
To THAT THOUGHT I FANTASIZE

In my LIFE
Your LOVE IS THE MOST PRECIOUS
THING I CALL my OWN

In my ARMS
Just WAIT TILL
you come
HOME —

♥R♥

Dearest Joan,

my LOVER
my HEART
my FRIEND
my PARTNER
my BEAUTY
my SOUL
my MOST CHERISHED
my MOST WANTED
my MOST DESIRED
my LADY
my LOVE
my LIFE

— HAVE A NICE DAY —

— LOVING you —
x
♡
Richard
♡   x x

Printed in the United States
By Bookmasters